T0008961

ZERO F*CKS GIVEN

Published in 2023 by OH!
An imprint of Welbeck Non-Fiction Limited, part of Welbeck Publishing Group. Offices in London, 20 Mortimer Street, London W1T 3JW, and Sydney, 205 Commonwealth Street, Surry Hills 2010.
www.welbeckpublishing.com

Text and Design © Welbeck Non-Fiction Limited 2023
All images: Shutterstock/zubarevid

Disclaimer: All trademarks, copyright, quotations, company names, registered names, products, characters, logos and catchphrases used or cited in this book are the property of their respective owners. This book is a publication of *OH! An imprint of Welbeck Non-Fiction Publishing* and has not been licensed, approved, sponsored, or endorsed by any person or entity.

All rights reserved. No part of this publication may be reproduced, stored in a retrieval system, or transmitted in any form or by any means (including electronic, mechanical, photocopying, recording, or otherwise) without prior written permission of the copyright owners and the publisher.

A CIP catalogue record for this book is available from the British Library.

ISBN 978-1-83861-182-8

Publisher: Lisa Dyer
Compilation and writing: Katie Hewett
Design: Lucy Palmer
Production: Felicity Awdry

Printed and bound in Dubai

10 9 8 7 6 5 4 3 2 1

ZERO F*CKS GIVEN

BADASS QUOTES FOR STRONG WOMEN

CONTENTS

3 I MAKE THE RULES 78 →

4 STAY OUT OF MY WAY 124 →

5 I'M OVER IT 156 →

Are you fed up with being taken for granted, undervalued, underappreciated and underestimated? Do you sometimes just want to do things your way and to hell with everyone else? Do you want to say what you think without worrying about the consequences? Look no further – you have found your tribe.

Zero F*cks Given is a collection of slogans and quotes by tough-talking women, from boss b*tches, badass babes, awesome authors and the sassiest superstars from past and present – the sisters who tell it like it is and take no prisoners. Each of the five chapters gets right to the heart of what bothers you the most and leaves everyone in no doubt about how you may be feeling.

The first chapter, I Am Who I Am, is for all those who proudly own who they are, embracing their flaws and making no apologies. Don't Give a Damn! celebrates honesty, straight talking and being brave enough to give as good as you get. I Make the Rules is advice on how to shape your own life, think creatively and lead life your way. Stay Out of My Way is a warning to anyone who tries to stop you from reaching your fullest potential – you will get there or die trying. Finally, I'm Over It is for everyone who is tired of being diminished, unheard and misunderstood – for those who have really had enough.

Full of attitude, brimming with confidence, ready for a fight and utterly unafraid, this is the book for women for whom there are

ZERO F*CKS GIVEN!

I AM
WHO I AM

This chapter is for all those who choose to lead not follow, to assert their voice, their opinions, their needs. To refuse to allow others to define, undermine, intimidate or second-guess them.

Take inspiration from the wise words of other women and be brave enough to tell (and show) the world who you are in all your glory— proud, noble, fierce and full of possibility.

66

Think like a queen. A queen is not afraid to fail. Failure is another stepping-stone to GREATNESS.

99

Oprah Winfrey,
presenter, actor and producer

"

STRONG WOMEN

DON'T HAVE

'ATTITUDES',

WE HAVE

STANDARDS.

"

Marilyn Monroe

"

There's something special about a woman who dominates in a man's world. It takes a certain grace, strength, intelligence, fearlessness, and the nerve to never take no for an answer.

"

Rihanna, singer and businesswoman

66

I am woman phenomenally. PHENOMENAL woman, that's me.

99

Maya Angelou, author

"

Let go of who you think you're supposed to be; embrace who you are.

"

Brené Brown, lecturer and author

> **"**
> # There is no gate, no lock, no bolt that you can set upon the freedom of my mind.
> **"**

Virginia Woolf, *A Room of One's Own* (1929)

I'M TOUGH, AMBITIOUS, and I know exactly what I want. If that makes me a b*tch, okay.

Madonna, singer

66

The sooner you understand that you don't have to be everyone's friend, the better off you'll be.

99

Andi Zeisler, Mashable, March 2016

"

Be the type of girl that climbs the ladder wrong by wrong.

"

Mae West, actor

66

You could certainly say that I've never underestimated myself, there's nothing wrong with being AMBITIOUS.

99

Angela Merkel, politician

"

Each time a woman stands up for herself, without knowing it possibly, without claiming it, she stands up for all women.

"

Maya Angelou, poet

So here is the quick way of working out if you're a feminist. Put your hand in your pants. a) Do you have a vagina? and b) Do you want to be in charge of it? If you said "yes" to both, then **congratulations! You're a feminist.**

Caitlin Moran, journalist

"

Leave it to me: I'm always top banana in the shock department.

"

Holly Golightly, *Breakfast at Tiffany's* (1961)

"

Be a lady?
FORGET IT.
Ladies don't last a day in the real word. No one's a lady anymore. Why do you think we get our claws polished?

"

Crystal Woods, author

I'M NOT RUDE.
I'M JUST SAYING
WHAT EVERYONE
ELSE IS THINKING.

"

There is a stubbornness about me that never can bear to be frightened at the will of others. My courage always rises at every attempt to intimidate me.

"

Lizzie Bennett, Jane Austen's *Pride and Prejudice* (1813)

"

BE MESSY

and complicated

and afraid and

show up anyways.

"

Glennon Doyle Melton, author

TAKE CONTROL OF THE NARRATIVE

The most influential thing another woman has ever taught me is that my womanhood is personal and that I am in control of my own narrative. How I define and represent myself as a woman is completely up to me, and I should avoid being influenced by those who don't have to walk in my shoes.

It's one thing to be inspired by others and learn from them — that's how we grow and form our own identities. It's another to allow others to define your womanhood for you, because it often means living a life that makes others comfortable rather than one that empowers you.

**Feminista Jones (Michelle Taylor),
sex-positive feminist writer and activist,
Mashable, 2016**

"

The first thing I do in the morning is brush my teeth and sharpen my tongue.

"

Dorothy Parker, writer, critic and satirist

66

I will not be judged by you or society. I will wear whatever and blow whomever I want as long as I can breathe – and kneel.

99

Samantha Jones, *Sex and the City*

I AM MY ROLE MODEL. I WANT TO BE ME.

"

Don't give up, don't take anything personally, AND DON'T TAKE NO FOR AN ANSWER.

"

Sophia Amoruso,
author and businesswoman

"

I finally got my answer to that question: Who do you think you are?

I AM WHOEVER I SAY I AM.

"

America Ferrera, actor

OUTSIDE THE BOX IS WHERE I LIVE

Kara Thrace,
Battlestar Galactica

66

WE'RE ALWAYS BLUFFING, PRETENDING WE KNOW BEST, WHEN MOST OF THE TIME WE'RE JUST PRAYING WE WON'T SCREW UP TOO BADLY.

99

Jodi Picoult, author

66

Wild women are an unexplainable spark of life. They ooze freedom and seek awareness, they belong to nobody but themselves, yet give a piece of who they are to everyone they meet.

99

Nikki Rowe, author

"

I'm an ice queen, I'm the sun king, I'm an alien fleeing from District 8 and I'm a dominatrix. So, I reckon that makes me lukewarm royalty with a whip from outer space.

"

Anna Wintour, *Vogue* editor,
Glamour, May 2017

66

I have insecurities, of course, but I don't hang out with anyone who points them out to me.

99

Adele, singer

"

Well, that's your opinion, isn't it? And I'm not about to waste my time trying to change it.

"

Lady Gaga, singer-songwriter and actor

66

BE YOURSELF. YOU'RE OKAY.

AND IT REALLY DOESN'T MATTER WHAT OTHER PEOPLE THINK.

99

Taylor Schilling, actor

66

If I make a fool of myself, who cares? I'M NOT FRIGHTENED by anyone's perception of me.

99

Angelina Jolie, actor

66

I can't think of any better representation of beauty than someone who is UNAFRAID to be herself.

99

Emma Stone, actor

"

I think you just have to do you, whatever that is, and not feel like you have to be a certain way for other people to like you –
THAT'S BULLSH*T.

"

Michaela Coel, screenwriter and actor

66

Responsibility to yourself means refusing to let others do your thinking, talking and naming for you; it means learning to respect and use your own brains and instincts.

99

Adrienne Rich, poet

DON'T GIVE A DAMN !

Learn how to CARE LESS! Lead from the front and avoid giving headspace and airspace to what others think or say about you. Slay the haters, bullies and oppressors by being brutally honest about who you are and what you believe. Never apologize for putting your ideas, opinions and thoughts above another's.

Live by the old adage that if you wouldn't invite someone into your home, why would you invite them into your head?

66

I have chosen to no longer be apologetic for my femaleness and my femininity. And I want to be respected in all of my femaleness because I deserve to be.

99

Chimamanda Ngozi Adichie, author

I HAVE AN ATTITUDE BECAUSE I HAVE EARNED IT

"

You can't please everyone, and you can't make everyone like you.

"

Katie Couric, journalist

EMBRACE IMPERFECTION

I embrace the label of bad feminist because I am human. I am messy. I'm not trying to be an example. I am not trying to be perfect. I am not trying to say I have all the answers. I am not trying to say I'm right. I am just trying – trying to support what I believe in, trying to do some good in this world, trying to make some noise with my writing while also being myself.

Roxane Gay, writer and social commentator, *Bad Feminist* (2014)

IMPERFECTION IS BEAUTY, MADNESS IS GENIUS, AND IT'S BETTER TO BE ABSOLUTELY RIDICULOUS THAN ABSOLUTELY BORING

"

I DON'T CARE WHAT YOU THINK ABOUT ME.

I don't think about you at all.

"

Coco Chanel, fashion designer

"

It's really liberating to

SAY 'NO'

to shit you hate.

"

Hannah Horvath, *Girls*

IT'S NOT THAT I DON'T LIKE YOU ... OH WAIT, YES IT IS

"

I JUST WANT TO BE MYSELF, AND I REALLY CAN'T SAY I'M SORRY FOR IT. I JUST CAN'T.

"

Aidy Bryant, actor and comedian

"

I have a horrible feeling that I'm a greedy, perverted, selfish, apathetic, cynical, depraved, morally bankrupt woman who can't even call herself A FEMINIST.

"

Fleabag, *Fleabag*

DO WHAT'S IN YOUR SELF-INTEREST

Learning to say no isn't always easy, but it is an adequate one-word response and you don't have to give lengthy reasons or excuses why you are turning something down. The Crunk Feminist Collective (March 2011) has some great advice to help you.

1 Don't let "Yes" be your default answer. Say "No" first. Its easier to go back later and say yes, than it is to go back and say no.

2 Never agree to do something on the spot. Always take some time to think about it and consider whether or not it is going to be an imposition.

3 Limit yourself to what you say "Yes" to, say three social events a month.

4 Never compromise your peace.
If you have a full plate, don't agree
to do something that will stretch you
beyond your limits. You do not owe
anybody anything.

5 Save "yeses" for yourself. Self-care is not
selfish. Don't say yes to something that
says no to you.

6 Don't apologize for saying no.
It's your right.

7 You can change your mind.
Circumstances may change
and your obligation is to yourself.

"

I think if you can dance and be free and not be embarrassed, you can RULE THE WORLD.

"

Amy Poehler, writer,
actor and comedian

"

THE IMPORTANT THING IS NOT WHAT THEY THINK OF ME, BUT WHAT I THINK OF THEM.

"

Queen Victoria

"

IF YOU OBEY ALL THE RULES, YOU MISS ALL THE FUN.

"

Katharine Hepburn, actor

"

Oh,
I wish
I could,
BUT
I DON'T
WANT TO.

"

Phoebe Buffay, *Friends*

YOUR OPINION
IS OF NO CONSEQUENCE
TO ME, BECAUSE
I KNOW I AM
AWESOME

"

If they don't like you for being yourself, be yourself even MORE.

"

Taylor Swift, singer-songwriter

" KNOW WHAT? BITCHES GET STUFF DONE. "

Tina Fey,
actor, writer and comedian

" "

No woman gets an orgasm from shining the kitchen floor.

" "

Betty Friedan, author and activist,
The Feminine Mystique (1963)

66

WHISKY, GAMBLING and FERRARIS are better than housework.

99

Françoise Sagan, writer

66

You're a woman with a brain
and reasonable ability.
Stop whining and find

SOMETHING
TO DO.

99

Violet Crawley, *Downton Abbey*

"

I don't need to 'use my body for attention' honey ... my talent already does that.

"

Lizzo, singer

66

I never regret anything. Because every little detail of your life is what made you into who you are in the end.

99

Drew Barrymore, actor

66

I KNOW WHAT YOU'RE FEELING DARLING, BUT REALLY, I DON'T EVEN CARE.

99

Patsy, *Absolutely Fabulous*

"

Why should I care what other people think of me? I AM WHO I AM. And who I wanna be.

"

Avril Lavigne, singer

"

NEVER RETRACT, NEVER EXPLAIN, NEVER APOLOGIZE.

Just get things done and let them howl.

"

Nellie McClung,
author, politician and activist

> **66**
>
> **Bravely, I broke the silence.**
> **I boldly shared the truth.**
> **I empowered myself to**
> **create healthy boundaries.**
>
> # I BECAME
> # A BADASS.
>
> **I no longer tolerated being**
> **shamed, blamed and manipulated.**
>
> **99**

Dana Arcuri, author, *Soul Cry* (2020)

" BAD DECISIONS MAKE GOOD STORIES. "

Ellis Vidler, author

66

Don't hold back because you think it's unladylike. We shouldn't be shamed out of our anger. We should be using it. Using it to make change in our own lives, and using it to make change in the lives around us.

99

Jessica Valenti, writer

"

You can't make people love you, but you can make them FEAR YOU.

"

Blair Waldorf, *Gossip Girl*

"It's not your job to like me, IT'S MINE.

Byron Katie, author

I MAKE
THE RULES

Don't hang back in the wings waiting for someone to hand you your Oscar. You don't need anyone's permission to step up and realize your potential.

Write your own rule book and build the life you want right now. All that praise, success, validation – it all comes from within you.

You make the rules.

"

Don't think about making women fit the world — think about making the world fit women.

"

Gloria Steinem, journalist and activist

"

Never do anything by halves if you want to get away with it. BE OUTRAGEOUS. Go the whole hog. Make sure everything you do is so completely crazy it's unbelievable.

"

Matilda, *Matilda*

The beauty of being a feminist is that you get to be whatever you want. And that's the point.

Shonda Rhimes,
screenwriter, author and producer

"

In a world that wants women to whisper, **I choose to yell.**

"

Luvvie Ajayi, author

POWER'S NOT GIVEN TO YOU. YOU HAVE TO TAKE IT.

Beyoncé Knowles, singer

66

When I'm hungry, I eat. When I'm thirsty, I drink. When I feel like saying something, I say it.

99

Madonna, singer

I hear a lot of people saying, when talking about girls' empowerment ..., 'You're helping them find their voices.' I fundamentally disagree with that. Women don't need to find their voice. They need to feel empowered to use it and people need to be encouraged to listen.

Meghan, Duchess of Sussex,
Royal Foundation Forum 2018

66

I am a woman and a warrior. If you think I can't be both, you've been lied to.

99

Zeyn Joukhadar, author

"

I'd rather regret the things I've done than regret the things I haven't done.

"

Lucille Ball, actor

MAKE YOUR OWN RULES OR BE A SLAVE TO ANOTHER'S

66

It took me quite a long time to develop a voice, and now that I have it, I am not going to be silent.

99

Madeleine Albright, politician

"

If you don't risk anything, you risk even more.

"

Erica Jong, author

66

I may be wearing makeup, but I can throw a fastball by you at the same time.

99

Jennie Finch, softball player

"

EXPECT THE UNEXPECTED, AND WHENEVER POSSIBLE, BE THE UNEXPECTED.

"

Lynda Barry, cartoonist

I LOVE BREAKING THE RULES OF SOCIETY,

AND MAKING MY OWN!

I HATE CONFORMING TO THE HIGH STANDARDS OF MORALITY, SET EXCLUSIVELY FOR WOMEN!

Deeksha Tripathi,
50 Shades of Life and Me (2020)

66

You get to live your life the way you want. That's the whole point of not being in a bunker. NO ONE GETS TO TELL YOU WHAT TO DO.

99

Kimmy Schmidt,
Unbreakable Kimmy Schmidt

"

I do know one thing about me: I don't measure myself by others' expectations or let others define MY WORTH.

"

Sonia Sotomayor, lawyer

66

I would make a great queen because I am stubborn — if that's what I wanted.

99

Nakia, *Black Panther* (2018)

"

A strong woman looks a challenge dead in the eye and gives it a wink.

"

Gina Carey, author

66

Always keep your smile. That's how I explain my long life. I THINK I WILL DIE LAUGHING.

99

Jeanne Calment,
the world's oldest person

IF YOU WANT
TO LIVE, STOP
ASKING PERMISSION.
DO IT NOW
AND REGRET
IT LATER.

"

If I'm at a party where I'm not enjoying myself, I will put some cookies in my jacket pocket and leave without saying goodbye.

"

Mindy Kaling, actor

"

You know my code: hos before bros, uteruses before duderuses, ovaries before brovaries.

"

Leslie Knope, *Parks and Recreation*

66

Man may have discovered fire, but women discovered how to play with it.

99

Candace Bushnell,
journalist and author

TELL ME NOT
TO DO SOMETHING
AND I WILL
DO IT TWICE AND
TAKE PICTURES

"

Sometimes you gotta be a beauty and a beast.

"

Nicki Minaj, singer

"

That's only okay when I say it.

"

Janis Ian, *Mean Girls* (2004)

I AM NOT ARGUING.
I'M ACTIVELY
EXPLAINING
WHY I AM
RIGHT.

I DON'T LOOK BACK UNLESS THERE IS A GOOD VIEW

66

I've always done WHATEVER I WANT and always been EXACTLY WHO I AM.

99

Billie Eilish, singer

"

Life is either a daring adventure or nothing. Security does not exist in nature, nor do the children of men as a whole experience it. Avoiding danger is no safer in the long run than exposure.

"

Helen Keller, disability rights advocate

"

AS LONG AS I HAVE ONE ASS INSTEAD OF TWO, I'LL WEAR WHAT I LIKE.

"

Erin Brockovich, *Erin Brockovich* (2000)

66

You can do one of two things: just shut up, which is something I don't find easy, or learn an awful lot very fast, which is what I tried to do.

99

Jane Fonda, actor

> **You can be a thousand different women. It's your choice which one you want to be. It's about freedom and sovereignty. You celebrate who you are. You say,**
>
> # 'THIS IS MY KINGDOM.'

Salma Hayek, actor

"

IF YOU WANT IT, AND THE MORE YOU KEEP HEARING YOU CAN'T HAVE IT, YOU JUST GO AND GET IT.

"

Cardi B, singer

"

If you plan to build walls around me, know this – I will walk through them.

"

Richelle E. Goodrich, author,
Making Wishes (2015)

BREAKING THE RULES TO BREAK BARRIERS

According to an article by behavioural scientist Francesca Ginno, in *Harvard Business Review* in May 2018, there are four ways you can break the rules and in doing so break some barriers.

1 When approaching a high-stakes situation like a job interview, a presentation or even a first date, instead of telling yourself to calm down and relax, frame your nervous energy as excitement.

2 Own your femininity. Instead of a problematic sterotype, the "feminine" quality of warmth can be an opportunity as it makes you a more resilient and effective leader.

3 Keep breaking rules. You're supposed to know it all? Admit what you don't know and ask for advice – this earns respect.

4 Make your own rules whenever you get a chance. Fight against the attitudes and roles imposed by society, seizing every opportunity to prove them wrong.

" I mean, it's sort of exciting isn't it? BREAKING THE RULES. "

Hermione Granger, *Harry Potter and the Order of the Phoenix* (2003)

Our deepest fear is not that we are inadequate. Our deepest fear is that we are powerful beyond measure. It is our light, not our darkness, that most frightens us. We ask ourselves, "Who am I to be brilliant, gorgeous, talented, fabulous?"

Actually, who are you not to be?

Marianne Williamson,
author and activist

"

I attribute my success to this: I never gave or took any excuse.

"

Florence Nightingale,
nurse and social reformer

66

I am no longer accepting the things I cannot change. I am changing the things I cannot accept.

99

Angela Davis, author and activist

A STRONG WOMAN
is a woman determined
to do something others
are determined
not be done.

Marge Piercy, poet

"

The norms were created by somebody, and each of us is somebody. WE CAN MAKE OUR OWN NORMAL.

"

Glennon Doyle, author,
Untamed (2020)

STAY OUT
OF MY WAY

For women who aren't afraid to kick ass, here's some inspiration for breaking those glass ceilings and fighting off challenges, from whichever direction they come. Know your power and how to maximize it and be ready to change direction if the situation demands.

Don't listen to the detractors or those who try to hold you back or sideline you. The world is yours for the taking and you know what is best for you.

BE
SAVAGE
NOT
AVERAGE

Women are leaders everywhere you look – from the CEO who runs a Fortune 500 company to the housewife who raises her children and heads her household. Our country was built by strong women, and we will continue to break down walls AND DEFY STEREOTYPES.

Nancy Pelosi, politician

"

Drama is very important in life: you have to come on with a bang. You never want to go out with a whimper.

"

Julia Child, cook and author

You think I'm just a doll.

A doll that's pink and light.

A doll you can arrange any way you like.

YOU'RE WRONG. VERY WRONG.

What you think of me is only a ghost of time.

I AM DANGEROUS.

AND I WILL SHOW YOU

JUST HOW DARK I CAN BE.

Harley Quinn, *Suicide Squad* (2016)

"

If I stop to kick every barking dog I am not going to get where I'm going.

"

Jackie Joyner-Kersee, athlete

For I conclude that the enemy is not lipstick, but guilt itself; we deserve lipstick, if we want it, AND free speech; we deserve to be sexual AND serious – or whatever we please. WE ARE ENTITLED TO WEAR COWBOY BOOTS TO OUR OWN REVOLUTION.

Naomi Wolf, author and activist

"

SUCCESS IS GETTING
WHAT YOU WANT;
HAPPINESS IS WANTING
WHAT YOU GET.

"

Ingrid Bergman, actor

> **"**
>
> **I don't perform miracles or do the impossible. I make cold calculations about difficult situations, and I do not take on anything I know I won't win.**
>
> **AND I WILL WIN THIS.**
>
> **"**

Olivia Pope, *Scandal*

"

And when they dare to tell you about

all the things you cannot be,

you smile and tell them,

I am both war and woman and
YOU CANNOT STOP ME.

"

Nikita Gill, writer

"

Option A is not available. So let's KICK THE SH*T out of option B.

"

Sheryl Sandberg,
businesswoman and philanthropist

"

We know that when a
woman speaks truth
to power, there will be
attempts to put her down
... I'M NOT GOING
TO GO ANYWHERE.

"

Maxine Waters, politician

66

Behind every great man is a woman with blood on her hands.

99

Claire Underwood, *House of Cards*

SILENCE IS POWER

When people are insulting you, there is nothing so good for them as not to say a word — just to look at them and think. When you will not fly into a passion people know you are stronger than they are, because you are strong enough to hold in your rage, and they are not, and they say stupid things they wished they hadn't said afterward. There's nothing so strong as rage, except what makes you hold it in — that's stronger. It's a good thing not to answer your enemies.

Sara Crewe, in Frances Hodgson Burnett's
A Little Princess **(1905)**

UNDERESTIMATE ME? THAT'LL BE FUN

66

SMILE AND SLAY.

You have to slay it in life or life will slay you.

99

Janna Cachola,
actor, singer and model

"

The most effective way to do it,

IS TO DO IT.

"

Amelia Earhart, aviation pioneer

66

My mad face and my happy face are the same.

99

Pamela Swynford, *True Blood*

YOU ARE EITHER
ON MY SIDE,
BY MY SIDE OR
IN MY
F*CKING WAY.
CHOOSE WISELY.

"

There are two powers in the world: one is the sword and the other is the pen. There is a third power stronger than both, THAT OF WOMEN.

"

Malala Yousafzai, education activist

"

IF I BE WASPISH, BEST BEWARE OF MY STING.

"

Katherine, in *The Taming of the Shrew*
by William Shakespeare

"

I come in peace,
BUT MEAN
BUSINESS.

"

Janelle Monáe, singer and actor

66

I am a woman with thoughts and questions and sh*t to say. I SAY IF I'M BEAUTIFUL. I SAY IF I'M STRONG. YOU WILL NOT DETERMINE MY STORY – I WILL.

99

Amy Schumer, actor and comedian

"

I can be a regular b*tch. Just try me.

"

Lisbeth Salander, in Stieg Larsson's *The Girl with the Dragon Tattoo* (2005)

Someone telling me that I should stay in my lane or keep my mouth shut about things I don't know about — y'all don't know what you're talking about. I keep myself updated. I keep myself educated.

Lauren Jauregui, singer-songwriter

66

Often times, the most RIGHTEOUS thing you can do is shake the table.

99

Alexandria Ocasio-Cortez, politician

66

LIFE'S A BITCH.
YOU'VE GOT TO
GO OUT AND
KICK ASS.

99

Maya Angelou, poet

"

**COURAGE, SACRIFICE,
DETERMINATION, COMMITMENT,
TOUGHNESS, HEART, TALENT, GUTS.**
That's what little girls are made of;
the heck with sugar and spice.

"

Bethany Hamilton, surfer

OVERPOWER.
OVERTAKE.
OVERCOME.

Serena Williams, tennis player

"

I'm not
a humanitarian.
I'M A
HELL-RAISER.

"

Mother Jones (Mary Harris Jones),
activist and community organizer

66

I'm not going to stop the wheel. I'm going to break the wheel.

99

Daenerys Targaryen, *Game of Thrones*

I'M
OVER IT

Bad attitudes, negativity, toxicity, mansplaining and inequality getting you down? Feeling messed around and manipulated? People holding you to ideals that aren't your own? Yeah, you're over it and more ...

Here you'll find some ways to tell the world to back off without losing your sh*t , plus advice on letting go when you know you need to.

THERE IS A DIFFERENCE
BETWEEN GIVING UP
AND KNOWING WHEN
YOU'VE HAD ENOUGH

"

Women, they have minds, and they have souls, as well as just hearts. And they've got ambition, and they've got talent, as well as just beauty. I'm so sick of people saying that love is just all a woman is fit for.

"

Jo March in Louisa May Alcott's
Little Women (1868–69)

"

I got to the point where I was fed up with so many people telling me how and who I was supposed to be.

"

Estelle, singer

KEEP CALM AND PUT YOUR B*TCHFACE ON

66

When a man gives his opinion, he's a man. When a woman gives her opinion, she's a b*tch.

99

Bette Davis, actor

"

**I'd rather
set fire to my vulva,
so that's a**

'No'.

"

Selina Meyer, *Veep*

After all those years as a woman hearing "Not thin enough, not pretty enough, not smart enough, not this enough, not that enough," almost overnight I woke up one morning and thought:

I'M ENOUGH.

Anna Quindlen, author

"

I'm done with trying to be perfect. A perfect body belongs to someone else – and it's not me.

"

Geri Halliwell

66

Why is it that whenever a woman is strong and powerful, they call her a witch?

99

Lisa Simpson, *The Simpsons*

IF I ACT LIKE

I DON'T

CARE

THAT'S BECAUSE

I DON'T

KNOWING WHEN TO LET GO

You're over it, but you're still in it. Whatever it is
– job, romance, friendship – here are the signs
that it's time to say goodbye.

1 It feels unsafe physically or emotionally.

2 You are making excuses to stay in it or
excuses for another's behaviour.

3 You don't like who you are in the
relationship or situation.

4 Your energy is being drained and
your joy dampened.

5 You've outgrown them or the situation.

6 There's more bad than good.

7 People you trust are telling you
to get out of it.

8 You can't see a future happening.

9 There's no give and take –
the situation is unbalanced.

10 The trust is gone.

11 Your priorities and values aren't aligned.

"

Nobody has their sh*t together.
We are all one tantrum, door
slam, mismatched shoe or eye
roll away from questioning how
we are doing it every day.
BUT DAMN IT, WE ARE.

"

Sarcastic Mommy, Instagram

When I'm tired, I rest. I say, "I can't be a

SUPERWOMAN

today."

Jada Pinkett Smith, actor

THE MOST DANGEROUS ANIMAL IN THE WORLD IS A SILENT, SMILING WOMAN.

> **"**
>
> I don't put up with being messed around, and I don't suffer fools gladly. The short version of that is that I'm a b*tch. Trust me, I can provide character references.
>
> **"**

Robin McKinley, author

"

I can't do shit with
I'M SORRY.

"

Red, *Orange is the New Black*

I AM DONE
EXPLAINING
MYSELF.

MY STUFF
IS TOO
CRAZY FOR
BASIC PEOPLE.

WHEN ENOUGH IS ENOUGH

I'm finally learning to accept myself as I am. Learning to like myself as I am. Learning to like and accept my life as it is. Learning to stop begging people to want me or love me or make me feel like I'm **ENOUGH**. And learning that it's okay to stand up and say: I've had **ENOUGH**. I've had enough of hustling for my worth. I've had enough of groveling to people unworthy of me for scraps of love or time or attention. I've had enough of keeping people in my life who diminish me. And I've had enough of trying to be anything other than me ... because I, in all my imperfect, messy glory, am

PERFECTLY ENOUGH.

Mandy Hale, author,
You Are Enough **(2018)**

66

Hold your head high, and your middle finger higher.

99

Megan Fox, actor

SOME PEOPLE ARE LIKE CLOUDS. ONCE THEY ARE GONE, IT'S A BEAUTIFUL DAY.

WOMEN ARE COMPLICATED. WOMEN ARE MULTIFACETED. Not because women are crazy. But because people are crazy, and women happen to be people.

Tavi Gevinson, actor and writer

I'M GUILTY
OF GIVING PEOPLE
MORE CHANCES
THAN THEY DESERVE
BUT WHEN I'M DONE,
I'M DONE.

66

Letting go doesn't mean that you don't care about someone anymore. It's just realizing that the only person you really have control over is yourself.

99

Debbie Reber, speaker and author

66

Why should I care about keeping my life on a perfectly straight course when it kept throwing wild curves at me?

99

R. S. Grey, author

HOW TO GIVE LESS FUCKS

Hey, sometimes caring less takes work. If you're finding it hard, try taking this advice from Casey Rebecca, on siren.com.

1. Stop planning and surrender yourself to the Universe, karma, or great beyond. As Casey says, "You can't control this shit, man. Things are happening, with or without your consent."

2. Let it all go. The hurt, the shame, the anger, the feelings. Know that you experienced something, and now the moment has passed, and all those fucks are floating away.

3. Act like you don't give a fuck – Fake it 'til you make it!

4. Do something new. When something ends, something else begins.

5. Find a reason to be happy every day. As Casey says, "It's a big fuckin' world with a lot of weird/cool/awesome/beautiful/thought-provoking shit out there".

DEAR HATERS,
I HAVE SO MUCH MORE
FOR YOU TO BE MAD AT.
JUST BE PATIENT.

DON'T EVER UNDERESTIMATE THE ACTIONS OF A PERSON THAT'S FED UP. LAST CHANCES DON'T COME WITH WARNINGS.

WAYS TO TELL SOMEONE TO F*CK OFF

1. Your absence is required.

2. I wish we were better strangers.

3. There is nothing to be gained by further conversation. Goodbye.

4. Clearly ONE of us has made a mistake, and wasted the OTHER's valuable time.

5. All things must come to an end. Whatever this is must also come to an end. Enjoy your life.

6. Best of luck to you and hope life treats you the way you deserve.

7. Off is the general direction in which you should fuck. Kindly refrain from contacting me again.

8. I don't think it will be necessary for us to see each other again.

9. There are 171,476 words in the English dictionary but none describe how much I wish to hit you with a chair.

10. This isn't a good time.
In fact, never is a good time.

"

"Nolite te bastardes carborundorum."

[Don't let the bastards grind you down]

"

Margaret Atwood, *A Handmaid's Tale* (1985)

"

... the more we have to put up with, the less tolerant we get ...

"

Ruth Klüger,
author and Holocaust survivor

PLEASE CANCEL
MY SUBSCRIPTION ...
I'VE HAD ENOUGH
OF YOUR ISSUES.

"

I will no longer accept apologies from you, I WILL ONLY ACCEPT ACTION.

"

Sonya Parker, author

I'M SORRY, YOU SEEM TO HAVE MISTAKEN ME FOR A WOMAN WHO WILL TAKE YOUR SH*T